ABOUT T

Caroline Philpott and Alexis Willett run Tangelo House: online training in practical, intelligent communications and public engagement.

Caroline Philpott is a marketing, communications and engagement expert. She has crafted her expertise over 20 years of supporting private, public sector and non-profit organisations across the UK. Constantly at the forefront of public engagement, she's designed and delivered everything from localised, community-based activities, and driving uptake of stop smoking services, through to England's national programme of cancer awareness campaigns alongside Public Health England, the Department of Health and NHS England. She's also led public relations for a range of IT and telecommunications clients. After many years of devising and implementing complex projects and strategies for in-house positions, she now shares her knowledge and experience with others at the frontline of communications and public engagement to support them to make a difference.

Alexis Willett, also owner and director of Punch Consulting, has 20 years' experience in science communications, engagement and health policy, supporting organisations around the world. She's an award-winning author of a broad range of publications, including popular science books. Her work has featured in major media outlets including The Guardian, BBC Science Focus, The iPaper, The Observer, HuffPost, Psychologies magazine, The Bookseller and The Scotsman. She gained her PhD in biological science from the University of Cambridge, also holds MSc and BA (Hons) degrees, and was a lecturer at Anglia Ruskin University. She's an experienced media spokesperson and has appeared on the BBC, Sky News and CNN International, amongst many other TV and radio channels.

ALSO BY THE AUTHORS

Science Communication Made Easy - 50 Practical Tips for Success

By Alexis Willett:

Drinkology: The Science of What We Drink and What it Does to Us, From Milks to Martinis

How Much Brain Do We Really Need?

PUBLIC ENGAGEMENT MADE EASY

35 Practical Tips for Success

Caroline Philpott & Alexis Willett, PhD

Public Engagement Made Easy – 35 Practical Tips for Success

First published in 2020.

Copyright © 2020 Caroline Philpott & Alexis Willett

The right of Caroline Philpott and Alexis Willett to be identified as Authors of the Work has been asserted by them in accordance with the Copyright, Designs and Patents Act 1988.

All rights reserved.
No part of this publication may be reproduced, stored in a retrieval system, or transmitted, in any form, or by any means, electronic, mechanical, photocopying, recording or otherwise, without prior written permission of the Authors, nor be otherwise circulated in any form of binding or cover other than that in which it is published and without a similar condition being imposed on the subsequent purchaser.

www.tangelohouse.com

DEDICATION

For all the people who showed me the way.
C.P.

For all the public engagement practitioners who work tirelessly and creatively to meaningfully involve people and make sure their voices are heard.
A.W.

ACKNOWLEDGEMENTS

We would like to thank the many inspiring and dedicated individuals that we've been fortunate to work, collaborate and share conversations with across our careers. Some of you have led the involvement of others, some of you have generously given up your time to be the ones involved. All of you have been shining examples of how powerful public engagement can be and how, done well, it really can make an incredible difference.

CONTENTS

1. INTRODUCTION	5
2. WHAT IS PUBLIC ENGAGEMENT?	11
3. THE FIVE FUNDAMENTALS OF EFFECTIVE PUBLIC ENGAGEMENT	23
FUNDAMENTAL 1: BE PURPOSEFUL – What do you want to achieve?	29
FUNDAMENTAL 2: BE SPECIFIC – Who do you want to engage?	35
FUNDAMENTAL 3: BE FLEXIBLE – How will you involve your audience?	51
FUNDAMENTAL 4: BE OPEN – How will you cultivate a good working relationship?	59
FUNDAMENTAL 5: BE REFLECTIVE – How will you monitor and evaluate your activity?	65
4. LOOK BEYOND YOUR OWN WORK	79
5. PLAN AND PREPARE	85

1
INTRODUCTION

In recent years, there has been a significant rise in the number of organisations and individuals wishing to incorporate public engagement into their work. From universities wanting to foster a more open relationship with the communities around them, to not-for-profit organisations and charities wanting to utilise the experience and skills of supporters in developing key areas of work, to local public health teams wanting to work hand-in-hand with residents to tackle a range of issues in their communities.

Public engagement can take many different forms – community engagement, patient involvement, and citizen science, to name but a few – but, essentially, it's about engaging and involving people in a process of sharing information, knowledge and experience to achieve a mutually beneficial outcome. When it's done well, it can lead to amazing developments and contribute to all sorts of change for the better.

Involvement, two-way communication and building strong working relationships are the core features of public engagement. It takes patience, trust and effort to really make it work, so it may be tempting to skip it and just press ahead with your own ideas to save time. When you're at the very beginning of a piece of work, just the idea of involving others can raise all sorts of questions and concerns: Where do you start? How do you handle the input from someone else? Where will it lead? How do you manage the expectations of funders or stakeholders if the activity you've agreed on or parameters of your work change course? While it may seem overwhelming or confusing, it doesn't have to be. You just need to take it one step at a time and *Public Engagement Made Easy* is here to guide you along the right path.

Although people talk about public engagement a lot, what you see isn't always what you get. All too often, and too easily, it can fall into the trap of simply becoming one-way communication, and then you're missing out on the all the insights and benefits that real engagement can bring. Or sometimes people are just confused about how it differs from good, engaging communications.

If you want to make sure your path to public engagement is effective, there are some essential steps you need to follow to take you to your destination. This book aims to broaden your understanding of public engagement, as well as teach you the five fundamentals you need to get right when planning your own public engagement activities, if you want them to have maximum impact.

If you think your work might benefit from involving others, whether it's people in a particular community or location or those with experience of a particular issue, don't be shy. Take a leap, reach out and see what amazing things you can achieve together.

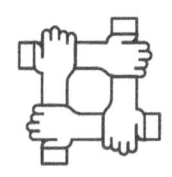

HOW TO USE THIS BOOK

Beyond the introduction, the book is divided into four further chapters that guide you through what public engagement is, the fundamentals that shape effective public engagement, and using the experience of others to make your activities even more successful. Practical tips are provided along the way, with the detail of each indicated by T.

If you are new to public engagement, we recommend that you work your way through the book from start to finish in order to understand how the fundamentals piece together. If you are refreshing your knowledge, or just wish to use the book as a handy reference on the different aspects of public engagement, you'll find that each fundamental is distinctly presented so you'll be able to dip in and out of it as you need.

For each fundamental, there is a short explanation of what it is, followed by practical and essential tips. The tips comprise a series of short points about the most important aspects to take on board, as well as questions to prompt your thinking and planning as you focus on that fundamental. There are also some short tasks to give you an opportunity to put the principles into practice as you develop your skills.

The tasks will require an example project to practise on. We encourage you to use a project of your own so you can build a plan for your public engagement activities. However, if you don't yet have a project, here are some example topics that you could use:

Example 1:
The creation of a research project to develop a new treatment for a disease

Example 2:
The design of a community-based health service

Example 3:
The redevelopment of green spaces in an urban locality

Example 4:
Fostering greater transparency of your organisation's work

At the end of the book, you will find a template worksheet to help get you started when planning a public engagement project. There are also notes pages for you to record your thoughts on the suggested tasks.

2
WHAT IS PUBLIC ENGAGEMENT?

In a nutshell, public engagement is an ongoing process of two-way communication between those leading an area of work and the 'public'.

Public engagement can mean different things to different people. Depending on what field you work in and what you're trying to achieve, the path of public engagement and the end result might vary greatly. Community engagement, patient involvement, citizen science, and co-creation are all associated with, or examples of, public engagement.

The 'public' or people you engage with will also differ widely from one project to another. They might be people in a particular community or place, people affected by an issue your work relates to, or people in a position of influence – be that in a professional capacity or as a volunteer advocate, they might be experts or non-experts. In many cases, your stakeholders (those with a vested interest in the issue or your work) and the people you need to engage with (a wider public) probably fall into several categories.

You might even have been part of someone else's public engagement yourself. Have you ever fed into a government consultation? Been a representative of some sort on a project or working group? Acted as a lay expert or patient advocate? Have you taken part in a campaign or activity to collate information, such as spotting types of clouds you see in the sky or logging a particular aspect of nature, like a certain insect or plant species, in your local area?

When you come across examples of public engagement, they may all look and sound very different, but there's one key thing that all good public engagement has in common - dialogue. No matter what form it takes, public engagement means reaching out to key people outside of your organisation and involving them in a process of sharing information, knowledge and experience to achieve a final goal.

Tip 1: Establish whether you want to carry out public engagement or just appealing communications

T: There can be confusion about the difference between public communications and public engagement. A common misperception is that by reaching out to the public through interesting communications you are also engaging them in your work. But this is still a one-way direction of communication, with the information and suggested actions decided by the campaign creator. A two-way relationship, enabling others to steer, and be a part of, what you develop is essentially what sets public engagement apart.

T: Public engagement is about building a productive relationship with your audience or stakeholders, creating a partnership and working together to achieve something that everyone involved will ultimately benefit from – it's a process of encouraging people to be interested in a more engaged way and be a part of what you're doing.

T: Whether you want to define your area of research, design a service to support people in key locations, or generate interest in or excitement about your work, the best people to help shape your thinking and guide you to success are the very people that are essentially going to be on the receiving end. They can help you make sure you're asking the right questions, delivering the most effective service or join you in making people take notice of your area of work or a key issue.

T: Here are some explanations of the types of public engagement and involvement we mentioned previously (as defined in the UK), most commonly used to support or shape an area of work. In this book, we use the term in its broadest context to incorporate all of these areas:

Public engagement: Although it's a term applied widely across a number of sectors (and we're using it in its broadest meaning), 'public engagement' is often used in the higher education and research sector to describe any communication and activities aimed at the public or non-specialists.

Community engagement: This involves working collaboratively with people in a particular 'community' to address their needs or ambitions. They might be in a specific geographic location, have a shared interest, or be in a similar situation.

Patient involvement: In this context, patient engagement and involvement refers to activities that encourage patients to take an active role in contributing to the design, planning and delivery of health services and research. The term is also used in relation to healthcare professionals involving patients in decisions about the management of their own health, treatment and care.

Citizen science: This is when members of the public participate in, or collaborate on, science research projects. These kinds of research projects are usually aimed at collecting or monitoring data of some description.

Co-creation: Also described as 'co-design', this is when public participants and/or stakeholders are involved in the design and development of something new, such as a service, product or solution to an issue. It's a very collaborative process, using the input and ideas of participants from start to finish.

T: You might hear 'outreach' mentioned in relation to public engagement. However, this is another field in itself that typically relates to projects or activities aimed at improving access to, and increasing participation in, services or programmes amongst a target group of people. As such, we don't cover guidance related to outreach in this book.

T: Communication can go a long way in raising awareness and imparting information, but even with the most targeted communications and clear calls to action, the people you're trying to reach still might not be interested or act. But if you involve them – ask what they think and feel, really listen to what they have to say and work with them, you're much more likely to successfully influence their thoughts, attitudes or behaviour. They're more likely to 'buy in' to what you have to offer if they feel part of it.

If you want to know more about communication, you'll find guidance in our companion book: *Science Communication Made Easy*.

TASK: Can you think of any examples of public engagement, good or bad? Are there any that you have been involved in? If so, what did you enjoy about them, or not like about them?

WHAT CAN PUBLIC ENGAGEMENT DO FOR YOU?

The first and most important question to ask yourself is this: how will your work benefit from public engagement or involvement?

Tip 2: Identify the benefits of public engagement for your work

T: Before you set out your aims or start thinking about who and how you're going to engage, you need to be really clear about how involving others in your work will make a difference and benefit your work. What value could others add? And what can you offer them?

T: This might also mean thinking about what your project involves, and when you might most value the input and feedback of others. For example, if you're a researcher, it might be at a very early stage, when you feel you could benefit from understanding the needs and experiences of people affected to define your focus. Or it might be at a later stage, when you've completed your research and need to engage with others to take it from an encouraging finding to a deliverable product, service or policy change.

T: It is often the case that your work could benefit from engagement at more than one stage. This is when it becomes even more important to invest time and effort in building strong, ongoing relationships with those involved. Whether it's to consult or collaborate, identifying the potential benefits and touch points are key to informing your aims and ensuring that whatever activity you undertake is true engagement.

T: Don't worry if you're partway through a piece of work or project, it's never too late to benefit from engagement.

TASK: Note down how you feel outside perspectives might benefit your project.

THE FIVE 'I'S OF PUBLIC ENGAGEMENT

Public engagement can come in many different guises, and the fine detail of each will vary widely, but there are five common features that define good quality, genuine engagement:

Involvement

Impact

Insight

Input

Ideas

The five 'I's are:

INVOLVEMENT: Proactively include key target group(s) in your work or project, either through consultation or collaboration

INSIGHT: Seek out and utilise the knowledge and experience of others to guide and inform your work

INPUT: Provide clear roles and opportunities for open, two-way communication to allow participants to fully contribute

IDEAS: Take on board the suggestions of participants to collaboratively develop projects or design activities

IMPACT: Monitor and evaluate all activity throughout the engagement process to ensure successful involvement and maximise the chances of achieving your outcomes

Tip 3: Put the five 'I's at the heart of your work

T: By making sure your public engagement activities incorporate the essence of the five 'I's, you greatly increase your chances of success and reaping the rewards.

3
THE FIVE FUNDAMENTALS OF EFFECTIVE PUBLIC ENGAGEMENT

In order to be a success, any kind of public engagement requires commitment and understanding of both the process and everyone who becomes involved in it. It's vital that participants feel valued and are kept informed for as long as they are involved in your work – to be able to share and learn from everyone effectively, it needs to be well thought through and properly planned.

Tip 4: Apply the five fundamentals of effective public engagement to ensure the best chance of success

T: There are five simple, but essential, steps along the path of public engagement. Get these right and you'll have a solid foundation for your work that you can build on in the direction that suits you. The fundamental steps follow a pathway and need to each be considered in turn.

The Five Fundamentals of Public Engagement

Be Purposeful — 1
What do you want to acheive?

Be Specific — 2
Who do you want to engage?

Be Flexible — 3
How will you involve your audience?

Be Open — 4
How will you cultivate a good working relationship?

Be Reflective — 5
How will you monitor and evaluate your activity?

Tip 5: Complete the journey and avoid shortcuts

T: Remember, this should be a two-way street between you and those who become involved throughout the whole process. It's not about simply getting from A to B via the straightest and quickest route.

T: You need to take in your surroundings, acknowledge and listen to the people around you. Sometimes you might need to linger for a while, or take a step back before you can take a stride forward. Although you will have a final destination, be that the end of a project or a key milestone in an ongoing piece of work, it's a path that will provide you with lots of lessons learned for the future – whether that's further engagement about your current work or a completely new project.

FUNDAMENTAL 1. BE PURPOSEFUL
What Do You Want To Achieve?

Having thought about how you could benefit from engaging with, and involving, others in your work, it's now time to get started. The first fundamental focuses on establishing a clear aim that outlines what you, as the project lead, want people to do, alongside what you want to achieve. In order to participate effectively and meaningfully, everyone involved also needs to understand what the ultimate destination or goal is, and what their role is in getting there.

Tip 6: Understand what category your engagement activity falls into

T: In order to take the most effective approach to public engagement, you need to ascertain how you want people to be involved in your project. And this means recognising what category of engagement you want to pursue. Broadly speaking, there are two main categories that most public engagement falls into: consultation and collaboration.

Consultation involves discussing your work or project with people to get their opinions or advice, and in turn using this input to help guide or inform it. For instance, using a key group of people as a sounding board for an idea or outline proposal you already have. You can then use this feedback to clarify or fine-tune the focus of your work.

Collaboration means working with those you engage with to create or achieve something together. For example, you may work closely with a group of people representative of their local community to plan, develop and set up a new service or resource.

T: *Information* (or to inform) is sometimes also listed as a form of public engagement. To inform is to impart news, facts or knowledge about your area of work. This can often be the approach with the most pitfalls - it's very easy to fall into the trap of 'broadcasting' one-way information, rather than engaging people with what you have to say. And even then, it's often just very creative, imaginative, and engaging communication. In order to be engagement, it would mean involving people in deciding what information to share and how. For example, a health professional might work closely with patients to create innovative resources, like a game or quiz, to share facts about a particular disease with people in their local area. However, done properly this approach to imparting information is either consultation or collaboration, drawing us back to our two main categories.

Tip 7: Set a clear aim for what you want to achieve

T: The first step to successful engagement is to establish a clear aim for the process. Your aim should be the overall goal. What do you want to achieve? What is the primary endpoint that you're hoping to reach? What do you want to happen as a result of your public engagement activity? Having a clear aim will help shape the direction and content of your activity.

T: In addition to defining what you want to achieve, it should also address what you want people to do. Is the aim to consult or collaborate? Do you want them to contribute as a one-off or throughout the life of a project? Do you want people to co-create or co-design an activity or service with you, or provide insight and feedback? Think carefully about why you want to engage with people and set out the broad parameters of their involvement as part of your aim.

T: Understanding what category your engagement activity falls into forms part of defining the aim of your activity. This element of your aim will feed into later decisions about who you engage with and how, so being clear about what you want from people's involvement at the very beginning is key.

Tip 8: Identify objectives that will support you in achieving your aim

T: Once you have decided what your aim is, how will you know whether you've achieved it? Now it's time to set specific objectives to describe what you want to achieve, how you plan to achieve it, and provide a framework for what the result of successful engagement will look like.

T: Objectives are steps that help break down the aim into specific, clear, measurable endpoints. Set some objectives that help define what you want to achieve, and that success can be measured against.

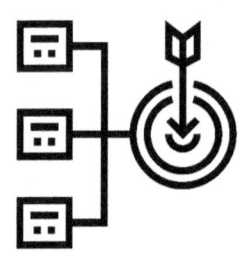

T: It's also important to be clear about timescales when developing your objectives, to support you in demonstrating how you're achieving your aim. Consider the short-, medium- *and* long-term outcomes of your public engagement. In the short term, it might be gathering insight or raising awareness, but the medium to long-term impact might involve driving people to take an action or change a behaviour, or improving a situation or service.

T: It sounds straightforward, but sometimes the difference between aims and objectives can be a bit confusing, so here's a very simplified example:

Imagine your aim is to get a new job in a new sector. Some examples of objectives to support you in achieving this aim might include:
a) Identify possible contacts in the new sector to gather further insight over the next two weeks
b) Identify transferable skills and scope areas of training required to increase your chances of success over next four weeks
c) Update your CV by the end of month one
d) Submit one application per week
e) Complete training course(s) to improve or develop any relevant skills by end of month two

Tip 9: Start planning how you'll evaluate the success of your public engagement activity

T: Now is the time to start thinking about how you are going to measure the impact of your efforts. Consider how you'll evaluate the success of your engagement activity. What will success look like?

T: There are lots of different ways to measure the outputs and outcomes of your activity. Some of these methods will be quantitative and others will be more qualitative. Some objectives might require a baseline - a measured starting point – before you implement your activity. We'll talk more about evaluation in the final fundamental, but it's important to start thinking about it from the start of any project. This will enable you to make sure that you put in place an aim and objectives that success can be measured against and identify any elements of your evaluation that may need your attention sooner than later.

T: Take time to consider how you will monitor the impact of your activity and progress against your key objectives along the way too, not just at the end.

TASK: Think about the key aim and objectives for your project. Do you want to consult or collaborate? What are the intended outcomes for your engagement?

FUNDAMENTAL 2. BE SPECIFIC
Who Do You Want To Engage?

The second fundamental is about identifying who you want, and need, to engage with. When you're planning any engagement activity, it's essential to consider who your target audience is.

Tip 10: Identify your target audience

T: A target audience is a group of people that will have most interest in what you have to say – they're the ones your project or the issue is most relevant to. It can be tricky to narrow down and define your audience and it may be tempting to believe that your work is relevant to everyone. But this is very unlikely to be the case and taking a one-size-fits-all approach to engagement is not effective and might ultimately fail to reach, or have an impact on, anyone.

T: The 'public' is a very big, diverse group – you can't engage with everyone and not everyone will want to, or be able to, provide helpful input unless it's applicable to them – so we need to break it down into smaller chunks. Remember, the people who can add the most value and share the most useful ideas will be those affected by, or with lived experience of, the topic or focus of your work.

T: Defining and segmenting target audiences can involve a variety of factors, depending on your work and what you are trying to achieve. Who might be affected by the issue or who would be particularly interested in it? Are there people who need to hear about the issue as they have the power to take action?

T: Does your area of work or the issue mean that you are looking at a very niche audience? Such as a group of patients with a particular health condition and lived experience of a specific treatment. Or is it a much broader audience that is made up of several different target groups? For instance, a range of people from different backgrounds or age groups within a local community that are all affected, in their own way, by the same environmental issue.

T: Are they affected by a particular issue? Community engagement projects often aim to deliver some kind of local support or benefit, be that health, social or environmental. In these scenarios, your target audience is determined by who lives in a specific area and/or is affected by a particular issue. If you wanted to develop a service for people aged over 50 at higher risk for a certain health condition, then that's who you should talk to. Input from people in their 20s wouldn't be particularly helpful, as how, when and why they would access a service is likely to be very different.

T: Or have they got something else in common, like a shared interest? You might work with people from your target audience to develop a citizen science activity or gain support not on subject matter, but by engaging people through something they enjoy doing. For example, a computer game that people play for fun but that has been developed to actually help identify something or understand an issue on a large scale. In this case your target audience for engagement might be gamers.

Tip 11: Do some research to make sure you're really aiming at the right audience

T: Is it 100% clear who your target audience is? You might need to gather more insight to be sure. This might come from data or information held in reports, or from other people working on the same issue or with the same groups of people.

T: You might know enough about your topic or the area you work in to identify who your key target audiences are, but you might need to do further research or gather more insight to really understand who you need to engage with. For example, if you have already done or planned some communications about your work, you might have some target audiences in mind. But don't just assume they will be the same for engagement activity. Look at your audiences and consider your engagement aims: is it the same or different target groups?

T: For instance, sometimes health promotion campaigns aimed at driving help-seeking or change of behaviour are actually targeted at 'influencers', such as children, partners or friends of those affected. The aim is to highlight the issue with someone who cares about the person affected and encourage these influencers to 'nudge' the person in the right direction. But if you then want to co-design a new service to support people affected by the issue, they themselves are the ones you need to involve (not the influencers). Think about who you need to engage with to achieve your desired result.

T: Even if the target audience for engagement is the same, ask yourself, does it need to be segmented further? For instance, to those in a particular location or a specific age group.

Tip 12: Get to 'know' your target audience

T: Identifying your target audience may sound like quite a lot of work and effort, but the more targeted you are with your activity, the more you maximise your chances of success. Understanding your target audience is essential for effective engagement. Spending time researching your target audience is an investment that will really pay out. The more you put into it, the more likely it is to deliver the impact you're aiming to achieve.

T: True public engagement benefits everyone – those driving it and the people, or audiences and stakeholders, participating in it. You've decided what you want and will gain from engaging with others. Now ask yourself: what's in it for them?

T: If you can see how a particular group of people would benefit from, or could support, what you're aiming to achieve, then there's a good chance that they are the ones you need to find a way to engage with. But even if people have a keen interest in what you are trying to do, say or address, they will need some sort of incentive or motivation to translate that into action – a willingness to give their time, energy and experience to engage with you in whatever way.

T: Once you've identified your target audience(s), you need to do research to understand their needs, preferences and interests. Put yourself in the shoes of your target audience and carefully consider: how they are affected by the issue; what their level of interest might be; what might inspire them to listen or get involved; what might encourage them to take action; and what the impact of their input could be.

T: Then you can think about what information, resources and other considerations your audience might need, or want, to get involved. The options are endless but by first considering who you are trying to reach, and why, you can choose the most appropriate content, style and approaches, tailored to your audience's needs, preferences and motivations.

T: Remember, no one is 'hard to reach' - you just need to understand how to engage with them.

Tip 13: Map out all of your stakeholders

T: It is also important to identify all your stakeholders. These are different to your target audience(s). Stakeholders are those with a vested interest in an area of work or project - not the people your engagement activity is aimed at. They can affect or input into your work, influence on your behalf or be influenced by it. They are usually both internal and external, for example, funders, suppliers, colleagues, partners, policy makers, end users, and so on.

T: You may have already started noting down some of your key stakeholders while thinking about your target audiences – often there are overlaps. Some of them might just need to be kept informed, some may be able to help you reach your target audiences, but some of them might actually be a target audience. The best and easiest way to determine their level of involvement is through a stakeholder mapping exercise.

T: Stakeholder mapping doesn't have to be complicated, and it can be incredibly valuable in thinking about how much or how little different stakeholders need to be engaged in your work. It involves listing all your stakeholders and then categorising them based on their potential level of interest and influence.

T: Below is an example of a community project with multiple stakeholders. Try making your own grid to decide on the level of participation required for each of your stakeholders. Select your key stakeholders from what you know about them and consider what role they play.

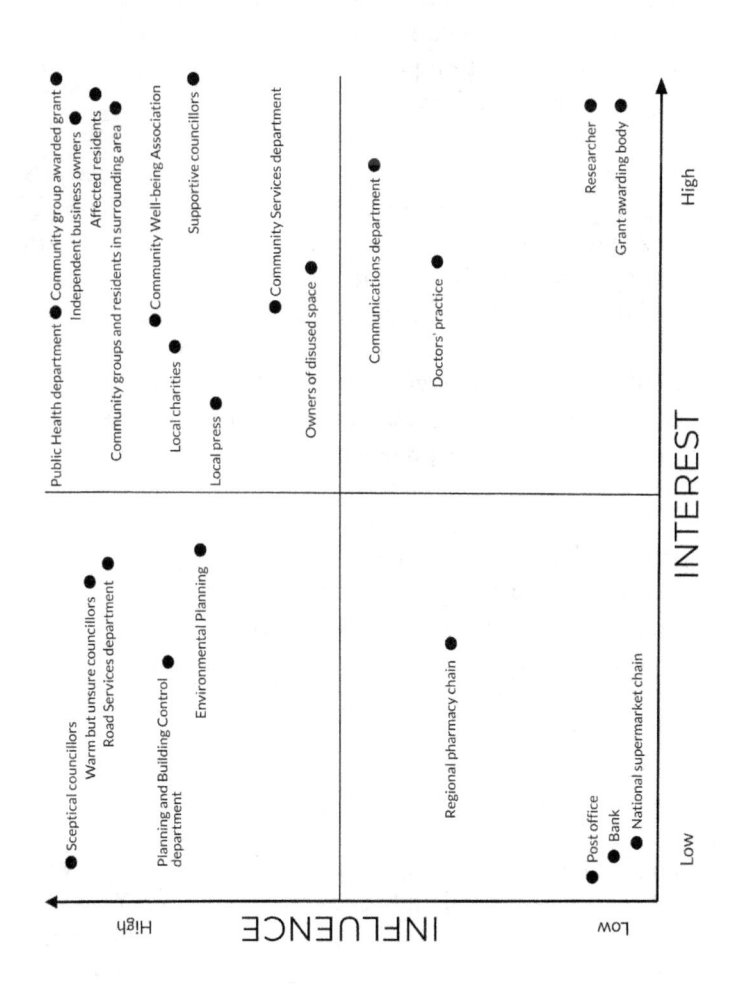

High Influence / High Interest:
- Public Health department
- Community group awarded grant
- Independent business owners
- Affected residents
- Community groups and residents in surrounding area
- Community Well-being Association
- Supportive councillors
- Community Services department
- Local charities
- Local press
- Owners of disused space

High Influence / Low Interest:
- Sceptical councillors
- Warm but unsure councillors
- Road Services department
- Planning and Building Control department
- Environmental Planning

Low Influence / High Interest:
- Communications department
- Doctors' practice
- Researcher
- Grant awarding body

Low Influence / Low Interest:
- Regional pharmacy chain
- Post office
- Bank
- National supermarket chain

Axes: INTEREST (Low → High), INFLUENCE (Low → High)

T: When deciding the level of involvement and priority of each of your stakeholders, consider: What is their level of interest? Would they benefit, directly or indirectly, from what you are hoping to achieve? If so, how would they benefit? Do they have any influence? How might you be able to use that influence? What level of involvement do you think they should have or might want in the project? For instance, input on plans, or promotion of, or show of support for, the project.

T: There is no right or wrong answer to this exercise. It's about getting used to thinking about the many people linked to or involved in a project, and how you will need to engage with them. Where each stakeholder sits on the grid will inform how you engage with them:

High interest and high influence: These are your key players to engage and you'll need to put the greatest effort into satisfying their expectations.

Low interest but high influence: These stakeholders have a lot of influence but not much interest, and they could even have the potential to be obstructive (such as a council representative opposed to the project, or senior manager from a different team who feels the budget should be spent elsewhere). These are the stakeholders you want to keep satisfied, so you will need to put work into anticipating and meeting their needs, but not so much communication that they tire of it or find it annoying.

High interest but low influence: These are the people with an interest in the project, but not much influence. You want to keep them informed, and they may provide helpful detail for your work, but they don't need to be heavily involved.

Low interest and low influence: This is your least important group of stakeholders because they don't have much interest or much influence – essentially, they just need to be monitored and provided with updates at a minimal level of contact.

T: Be as thorough as you can when identifying all the stakeholders for your work or project to make sure you don't overlook anyone. If you are concerned or suspect there might be a gap, why not check with colleagues or key people you have already reached out to?

T: Any map you create doesn't have to be set in stone. Things change and stakeholders may become more or less interested or influential over time. You may even want to try and nudge some of your stakeholders into being more interested or influential (which, in itself, will also require a plan!).

EXAMPLE: TARGET AUDIENCES

Here are two examples that illustrate how you might approach identifying your target audience(s).

Example 1: People affected by a particular issue

Imagine that you are planning a patient engagement project to develop a new community-based service. This service will provide a central 'one-stop-shop' to support people with a health condition that requires ongoing monitoring. The condition can be managed effectively through healthy lifestyle changes, which are known to improve a sufferer's day-to-day wellbeing in both the short- and long-term.

Your target audiences:

Patients currently living with the health condition in an identified local area, local patient support groups, care providers and relevant local health professionals. Patients will have a wealth of knowledge and experience of their condition, as well as current treatments or services, which you can gain valuable insights from. This is a service for them, so they are the key target audience.

How are they affected by the issue?

a) Patients might be struggling to make lifestyle changes without proper support, which is limited by lack of local resource. Services that do exist are all held in different locations by different organisations, which can be hard to access, particularly when patient's health is bad.

b) Care providers and health care professionals are limited by the amount of time and support they can give within the current system. They have concerns about the difficulty for some patients in accessing outside services, and how this might be a barrier to them being able to make changes that would improve their health and condition.

c) Local patient support groups do as much as they can but are limited by resource and the level of support they are able to offer.

What benefit would they get from participating?

All the target groups, especially patients, can help shape the service design – input into the kind of support they feel patients like themselves need, where and when they need it and so on. Patients and representatives from local patient groups could input into the specific kind of support or services they feel are required, have the opportunity to discuss issues with the current system and where they feel improvements could be made, or highlight things that work well and they would like more of. Care providers, health professionals and local patient groups can also provide input into what kinds of support would be most effective from a health benefit perspective.

What would the impact of their engagement be?

A high-quality service that will meet the needs of patients like themselves on a long-term basis; gives local carers and health professionals the reassurance that their patients will be able to access and receive all the support they need; and provides a clear referral route.

Example 2: People defined by a hobby, interest or lifestyle

Let's say that you're are planning a project to develop a health and wellbeing app aimed at busy mums of young children, who are often sleep deprived and lacking the time or opportunity to put themselves first.

Your target audience:

Mums of children aged three and under. Research has shown that mothers of children aged three and under are at particular risk of poor diet or under-eating, increased stress, excessive tiredness and increased consumption of alcohol. The majority of these women have smart phones, which provide them with a lifeline to friends, family and the outside world, and are frequent users of social media.

What benefit would they get from participating?

An opportunity to meet other mums and share experiences of the challenges of finding time for themselves. This has the potential for participants to get tips and advice from other mums in a similar situation, or similarly be a chance to help other mums who might be struggling during the engagement process. It's an opportunity for them to take time away from being a mum to do something for themselves and develop something they would hopefully benefit from in the long run. Depending on the activity, it might provide a socialising aspect that they might be otherwise lacking in their life.

What would the impact of their engagement be?

A useable app, informed by mums, that provides mums like themselves with the kind of prompts, information and support they need in a bite-size and quick to access format.

TASK: Start to identify your target audiences and key stakeholders for engagement. Who is affected by the issue your work relates to? Who has a vested interest in your project? Who will be able to provide valuable insight?

FUNDAMENTAL 3. BE FLEXIBLE
How Will You Involve Your Audience?

Finding the right approach and method of engagement is the focus of the third fundamental. You've identified who you want to engage, so now it's time to start planning how you will engage with them.

Tip 14: Put your target audience at the centre of your planning

T: Whatever method or approach you take to public engagement, it needs to be informed by your target audience.

T: Don't decide on a method or activity because it suits you or it's an idea you or your colleagues like. Think about the target audience's 'journey' to participation: you need to turn their interest into involvement, so the format has to be appealing and convenient to motivate and enable the right people to take part.

Tip 15: Don't expect people to come to you – you need to go to them

T: Think about where you will find your target audience, whether that's physically going to a location, online or otherwise.

T: Consider where and when to best engage with them, as well as how. If your target audience works during the day, then any activity might need to take place in the evening or at the weekend. If it involves people in a specific community or location, then that's where you need to be.

T: If you want people to participate, make it as easy as possible for them to do so, even those that are the most interested and motivated. Getting the format right is really important, but for face-to-face engagement in particular, location and timing are also key to success.

Tip 16: Look again at your stakeholders

T: Consider whether any of your stakeholders might be possible partners to support or assist you in delivering your engagement activity. Could they provide additional insight to help you shape your method or activity?

T: Look at whether they already have a relationship with the people you are trying to reach. If so, would they help encourage people to get involved?

T: Do any of your stakeholders have existing activities that you could piggyback on or utilise? If they already have an effective way of engaging with people representative of your target audience, think about how you might be able to use this as an opportunity for you to engage with them too, rather than coming up with something new that may take up a lot of unnecessary time or may not work as well.

T: Once you have engaged one or two key people in your target audience, would they be willing to act as an advocate and help you to reach additional volunteers? Think about how you can support them if they would like to get involved in recruiting others.

T: Start planning communications for your stakeholders alongside the activity planning. Take a look at your stakeholder map and think about who needs to know what and when.

Tip 17: Consider the wider context

T: Are there any contextual factors to take into consideration? What are the key priorities and needs within your field of work or the particular locality your target audience live in? Are there any particular opportunities or barriers? Perhaps there's a wider initiative that compliments your aims and objectives, or some sort of attitudinal barrier you need to consider before you can expect people to engage. Your work and your aims don't exist in isolation - consider what else is going on in your particular field or area of focus, and what impact that might have on what you want to achieve.

Tip 18: Familiarise your target audiences with yourself or your work

T: If your target audience is not already aware of you or your work, the initial stages of any activity planning will need to provide some background that introduces them to your field, your overall aim and how you feel their involvement could help shape your project or make it a success. This will help you gauge their level of interest and motivation to take part, as well as potentially provide insights into the best approach.

Tip 19: Plan the resources and input you might need

T: What needs to be in place to make your activity happen and who else needs to be involved in delivering it? This might range from physical resources and logistics, such as finding a sufficiently sized room or location, prompts for discussion, or catering, to human resource, for instance, other colleagues, a trained facilitator, a translator, a particular expert or community leader, or technical support.

T: Are there any other kinds of resource you need, like financial resource to provide expenses for volunteers or partners taking part, or processes put in place, such as security checks?

Tip 20: Make sure your involvement activity has a clear purpose

T: Agree some realistic outcomes to make sure it's a productive use of everyone's time. For example, if you are inviting people to a workshop to co-create something with you, or to a discussion group, you need to provide some degree of focus to keep things broadly on track. When there's a number of people all sharing ideas and making suggestions, it can be easy to go off on a tangent that might be less helpful.

T: Be open and upfront if there's any element of your project that participants can't influence or that is non-negotiable. People need to understand where and how their input is required.

T: Consider how to encourage people to think beyond sharing just their own views and experiences, especially if they're involved as a representative of a particular group. You want to hear what they have to say as an individual, but it's useful to get a wider perspective too.

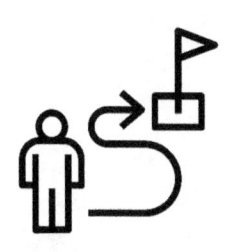

Tip 21: Ensure there's a clear and accessible mechanism for feedback

T: Feedback can provide valuable information about any areas for improvement in the project and help to continue building your engagement in the future. This will also likely feed in to the overall evaluation of your engagement activity.

T: How will people be able to feedback on their experience of taking part? Whether it's a one-off event or ongoing involvement over a period of time, you need to provide participants with opportunities to offer their perspective on the activity itself.

FUNDAMENTAL 4. BE OPEN
How Will You Cultivate A Good Working Relationship?

Once you've planned your approach and recruited members of your target audience to get involved, the next step is all about building a successful working relationship with them. Relationship-building is critical to effective public engagement and the fourth fundamental explores how to grow a good working relationship with a target audience into a strong, effective partnership.

Tip 22: Be patient

T: There are lots of things you can do to make sure that relationships grow into strong, effective partnerships, but the key thing is to be patient.

T: Remember that this is a two-way relationship. You need to listen, not tell or assume – everyone's input has value. You might be an expert in your field, but the very nature of targeted public engagement means you are involving people who are experts in their own way too. It's about working together to steer the path to your end goal.

T: It takes time to build trust, for people to settle into their role or feel comfortable with how, and how much, they are involved or share, and to get the process right. Try not to force it and help participants feel assured and supported in their role.

Tip 23: Set clear expectations and boundaries from the outset

T: Make sure you set defined roles and goals for people, so they understand where, when and how they can be involved.

T: Establish clear ways of working too. People need to be able to be involved as much, or as little, as they want to. They might have limited time to offer, or only want to be engaged at particular points. You need to allow for this, and being open about what input will be required for a given activity or role that will help both you and them manage this effectively, as well as support them in feeling comfortable with how they engage.

T: Put in place processes that will enable everyone to be heard in the process. Be clear when and how people can input, and find ways to encourage and support the most quiet, anxious or reticent participants to provide their thoughts. This will help to avoid particular individuals or organisations from dominating the conversation, as well as give confidence to others that they are being listened to and their input is equally valued.

T: If you're new to running interactive events, such as workshops or discussion meetings, seek guidance on techniques that help manage different personalities. There are books and websites full of information on ways to professionally address any challenging or dominating behaviours, or amplify the voice of the shiest people in the room, as well as ensuring you leave your own views and judgments at the door.

Tip 24: Pilot your activity

T: Depending on your type of engagement, it might be useful to pilot it on a small scale to see how people respond and participate. You can then use this experience and the feedback of those involved in the pilot to make any adjustments before you implement your activity in full.

T: Piloting activity might feel like it's just adding extra time or more work to your project, but again the key is patience. Taking the time to test your approach should be seen as an investment in getting the most out of your engagement activity in the long run.

Tip 25: Be adaptable

T: Once you do fully implement your planned activity, ask yourself: could anything be improved further? Is it as productive and effective as it could be? Keep adapting where necessary and appropriate.

T: Even if you had a successful pilot or had already made some changes to the original idea or format, delivering your activity on a bigger scale, or reacting to ongoing feedback, might mean you need to make further tweaks to activities.

Tip 26: Learn from, and respond to, feedback

T: It's important to hear feedback as you go along, and be able to learn from it and respond to it in the right way too. Remember that this two-way relationship includes you as well as your target audience.

T: Taking on board people's input doesn't mean you have to act on it, for instance if you feel its counterproductive or could take you too far off your path, but it does warrant your response. For example, explaining why you can't do or change something as they've suggested. In all likelihood, there is a compromise or something you can learn from it if you take the time to try to understand their point of view.

Tip 27: Keep everyone in the loop

T: Providing regular feedback to your target audience, such as about the impact of their input, about any key issues or about general progress and next steps, will also help grow your relationship. It shows that you are listening, that you appreciate their time and ideas, and see them as a partner in what you are trying to achieve.

T: Building relationships with people involved in your project will often be a very individual thing, but properly managing the engagement process, and being open and agile enough to adapt whilst keeping on track, will allow participants to see that you are learning from and acting on their input, and that you value their involvement.

T: If your project or activity includes an element of co-creation, it's even more important to manage the expectations of senior stakeholders, funders and so on from the outset and give them regular updates as your work progresses. It may be the case that something they have initially agreed to has to change to some degree in response to the input from your target audience. It will be vital to help them understand that this is part of the process in order to keep them on board, as well as keep them informed.

FUNDAMENTAL 5. BE REFLECTIVE
How Will You Monitor And Evaluate Your Activity?

Fundamental 5 is the final step on our path to effective public engagement. It focuses on the importance of monitoring and evaluation in demonstrating the impact of your work and gathering insight to inform future activities.

Tip 28: Allocate time in your project to enable a comprehensive evaluation

T: To successfully execute any kind of project, you move through a basic trinity of activities: you plan, you deliver, you evaluate. Typically, planning and delivery take up the bulk of your time and attention and it can be tempting to move straight on to something new once the project comes to an end. But good evaluation is the backbone of any well-planned, successful activity or project. It holds the whole thing together so you can see where it's working, where it's not and what the ultimate impact is.

T: Using feedback and evaluation mechanisms to monitor ongoing activity is particularly useful in public engagement. In fact, it's a key tool for ensuring that it's as effective as possible throughout the entire process. It will enable continued input from your target audience and help to flag up any areas for adjustment or additional consideration once your activity or intervention is live.

T: A thorough and well-considered evaluation provides the solid foundation for supporting and demonstrating success. It is vital in making sure that your engagement activity was effective in meeting your aims and objectives.

Tip 29: Follow the four main steps to meaningful evaluation

T: Step 1. Plan your evaluation from the start. Use a clear aim and specific, measurable objectives as the foundation for demonstrating the impact of your engagement.

T: Step 2. Use your plan to monitor progress. It can give useful feedback on how any activities are performing and provide opportunities to make adjustments along the way.

T: Step 3. Deliver your final evaluation. Paint a picture of how well your engagement activity went and what impact it had.

T: Step 4. Learn from your experience and inform future plans. Learn from what you did and found, and your experience of doing it, and use this to inform future public engagement activity.

Tip 30: Plan your evaluation at the outset of your project (Step 1)

T: Good evaluation involves measuring a range of outcomes that show the difference your activity has made, as well as the outputs of what you actually did. Those outcomes should relate to your set objectives, and you need to think about how you'll measure them at the outset of your project.

T: Depending on your area of work and the project, it's likely that you will have short-, medium- and even long-term objectives. Each of these will have a range of outputs and outcomes that you need to measure, and you'll need to differentiate between them as they each tell a different part of the story:

Outputs demonstrate what you actually did and what you delivered during your activity. For example: the number of focus groups or workshops you delivered, the number of participants in your activity, or the number of people accessing a service.

Outcomes show the impact of your activity or a measurable change that happened as a result of it. For instance: your workshops resulted in the co-design of a successful initiative that increased awareness levels of an issue, such as an increase in knowledge of signs or symptoms of a health condition. Or they resulted in the development of a new service and uptake of that service has driven an increase in the number of referrals for, or diagnoses of, a particular health condition.

T: There may be some outcomes that require a baseline to show the difference your engagement has made. For instance, if you want to show an increase in knowledge or levels of confidence, you need to know the starting point; in other words, what is the level of knowledge or confidence before your activity? If you don't already have this information, you need to consider how you will gather it before your activity starts.

Tip 31: Use your evaluation plan to monitor progress (Step 2)

T: Good evaluation is also about monitoring the impact of your activity whilst it's live. If something's not working, it can quickly let you know that something needs tweaking. And like anything good or worthwhile, the more you put in, the more you get out.

T: Without monitoring your work as you go along, there's the danger that you don't reach or involve the people you really need to, or that you waste time and resource repeatedly doing the same ineffective things. Best case, your activity just doesn't do anything or truly engage anyone, but worst case, it could cause more issues or misunderstanding.

T: You will need to have techniques and metrics to monitor your activity as you go along to enable you to adapt anything, if needed, and make sure it's as effective as possible.

Tip 32: Take an honest and objective approach when reflecting upon your work (Step 3)

T: When evaluating your engagement activity, keep an open mind and try to capture a fair picture of how well (or not) the project went. It's important to be honest in order to uncover what went well and what was less successful, and what can be improved in the future.

T: Your evaluation process should seek the views of everyone who took part, to fairly reflect its efficacy from all angles and aspects of the project. What might have seemed to be successful to you, might have been perceived as less successful by others.

T: There are a variety of ways to collect the data and insight you need to build a picture of the end results of your engagement activity. A combination of facts or hard data with more contextual and in-depth feedback will provide a well-rounded assessment. As well as the facts and figures, you want to be able to capture people's thoughts and feelings, opinions, experience, and levels of confidence too.

T: Here are some examples of techniques you might use to either assess people's involvement or measure elements of their experience of participating in your activity:

Pre- and post-activity surveys: These can help you provide a baseline for people's knowledge, opinions, and confidence levels before the activity and measure the differences afterwards. They might also enable you to understand people's expectations and find out whether they felt these were met. These kinds of surveys or questionnaires lend themselves to both overarching evaluation, as well as being a helpful method for measuring the impact of individual events or workshops.

Case studies and individual interviews: These can give you more in-depth insight into people's views or feedback on their experience of taking part in your project. If your activity means people are involved for a sustained period of time, or you are trying to show the ongoing impact of your work over a longer term, longitudinal case studies (which involve conducting in-depth interviews with participants weeks or months down the line) can provide an indication of whether the initial impact has been sustained, and how.

Feedback forms: These can offer a brief snapshot of people's experience of engaging with you. They could include a mix of quantitative questions measuring levels of satisfaction, as well as space for more qualitative feedback on any improvements you could make in the future. You could use these at regular time points or key milestones to help you monitor your activity.

Tip 33: Use the results of your evaluation to inform future work (Step 4)

T: A well-planned evaluation should also provide learnings for the future, either for yourself or to share with others.

T: Often, evaluation findings just sit in a report or presentation. Even if they're circulated amongst key stakeholders, they temporarily see the light of day but no one actually does anything with the information. An essential part of public engagement is not just getting it right and demonstrating that you did, it's about learning from the experience, using what your evaluation tells you, and taking those learnings forward.

T: Look at your results and consider how they could support or improve ongoing engagement activities – could you tweak anything to make it even better? What did you learn from the experience, what went well or less well, what might you do differently next time? What could you take from this experience into future public engagement projects?

T: Once you reach the finish line, it's also vital to let people know what you did and how you did it, as well as what you achieved. And not just those involved in your project, but a wider audience of peers, enthusiasts and people with a particular interest. There are lots of us out there 'doing' public engagement, or with an interest in it, which means there's a wealth of ideas, knowledge and experience to go around. Public engagement should benefit everyone: just think about everything you've learned on your journey and imagine what others could gain from hearing about it.

T: By sharing what you've learned and your experience – of the process, what went well (and, often more importantly, not so well), what you might do differently in future, what you would absolutely make sure you do again – everyone learns. You learn, your colleagues learn and others considering or undertaking engagement activities get to benefit from your experience too. All of which can only help to drive better, more effective public engagement all the way round.

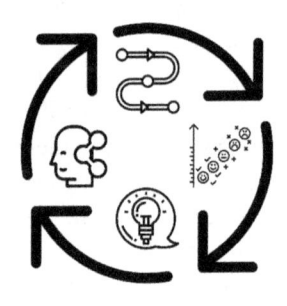

EXAMPLE: EVALUATION MEASURES

There are a number of ways to evaluate your activity, and how you choose to do this will depend on the nature of your public engagement and your intended goal. There may be outputs that you need to capture, as well as outcomes, but remember it's the outcomes that will demonstrate the effectiveness and impact of involving others in your work.

Output examples include:

a) Number of people attending an event or signed up to a forum
b) Number of people consulted about an issue or proposal
c) Number of workshops or sessions delivered

It's important to record and include these outputs as part of monitoring your activity, as well as your final evaluation, but they don't show what you have achieved. This is because the number of people taking part in a co-creation workshop, or consulted as part of a research project doesn't necessarily change anything – whether that's raising awareness, changing behaviour, designing a service or developing a research brief. While the involvement and input of these people might ultimately change or shape something, you will need to show that separately.

Outcome (or impact measure) examples include:

a) Change in awareness, knowledge, confidence and/or behaviour amongst your target audience from a baseline measurement (for example, captured via a survey before and after your activity)

b) Change in a strategy, policy, or key piece of legislation as a result of engaging successfully with influencers
c) Increase of service uptake by key target groups
d) Demonstrable impact on an area of research

TASK: Revisit the objectives you set for your activity. Identify what metrics you could use to measure them and consider how you will collect this information. How could you monitor these objectives and people's involvement as your project or activity progresses? What methods will help you achieve this?

YOUR CRITICAL CHECKLIST

We've now covered all the fundamental elements on the path to effective public engagement. When planning your own engagement activity, try to meet the following checklist to maximise your chance of success:

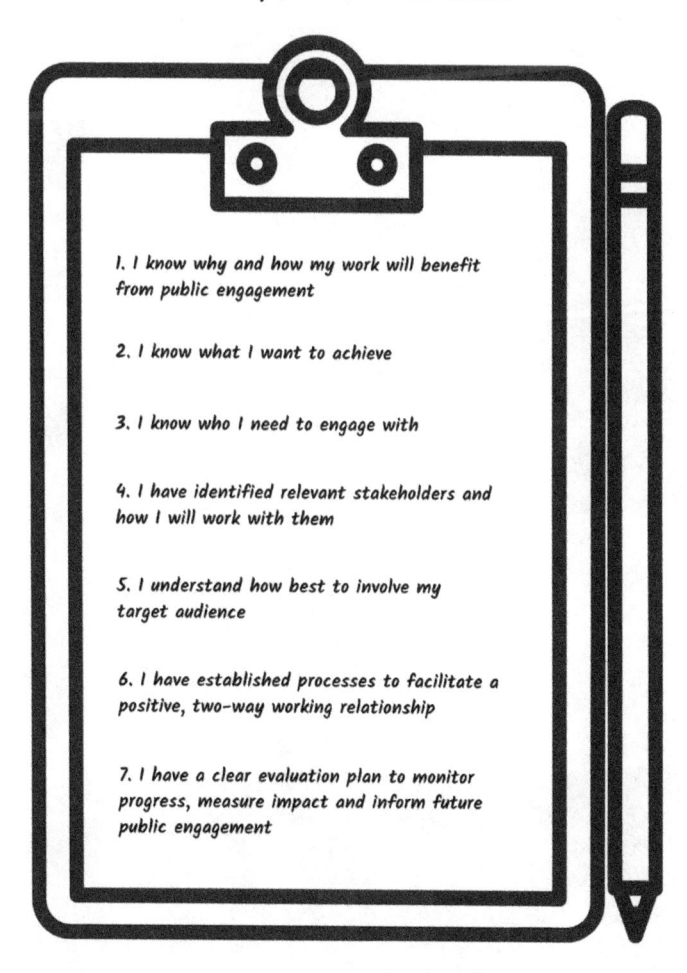

1. I know why and how my work will benefit from public engagement

2. I know what I want to achieve

3. I know who I need to engage with

4. I have identified relevant stakeholders and how I will work with them

5. I understand how best to involve my target audience

6. I have established processes to facilitate a positive, two-way working relationship

7. I have a clear evaluation plan to monitor progress, measure impact and inform future public engagement

4
LOOK BEYOND YOUR OWN WORK

Taking a look at the work of others inevitably makes us reflect upon our own work. It may give us confidence that we're on the right track or flag up where there might be gaps or issues, but often it can spark new ideas to make our plans even better.

Tip 34: Seek the expertise of others

T: There's no need to forge ahead by yourself and, in fact, this can often be detrimental. Asking others to share or input their expertise can be invaluable, so don't be afraid to ask for advice.

T: There are also lots of resources to support you with your public engagement work and, depending on the field you work in, there are many guides and examples. Take a look around for guidance relevant to your field or activity to support you in the planning and delivery of your project.

T: If you work in the higher education sector or research field, you can find a wide range of information, resources and in-depth training specifically aimed at supporting you. These include:

a) *National Co-ordinating Centre for Public Engagement* in the UK
b) *Wellcome Trust* – a UK-based foundation that supports researchers
c) *Engagement Australia* – an alliance of Australian and New Zealand universities focused on developing the engagement agenda in higher education
d) *Research Impact Canada* – a pan-Canadian network of universities committed to maximising the impact of academic research for the public good in local and global communities
e) *Sense About Science* – an independent charity that promotes the public understanding of science and challenges the misrepresentation of science in public life. This organisation has centres in the UK, EU and USA and also offers guides and information specifically for public engagement in research.

Most universities also have their own information and guides relating to public engagement.

T: A number of organisations offer support and resources to those involved in community engagement. For example:

a) *National Institute for Health and Care Excellence (NICE)* in the UK provides information on community engagement. 'Community engagement: improving health and wellbeing and reducing health inequalities' covers a range of recommendations and guidance

b) *Local Government Association* offers information and examples of community engagement across England, in relation to a range of issues, such as its publication: 'Integrating community engagement and service delivery – pointers to good practice'

c) *The Scottish National Standards for Community Engagement* are good-practice principles designed to support and inform the process of community engagement. It gives examples of many of the key principles needed to ensure community engagement is effective

d) *International Association for Public Participation* aims to advance and extend public participation and has communities of members in a number of regions around the globe, including Australasia, USA, Canada, Latin America and South Africa. As an overarching organisation and regional outlets, they provide tools, case studies and training to members.

There are other regional, local or specific guidelines out there to support you, depending on where you are and the field you work in, such as 'The Guidelines for Public Engagement 2019' by Health Canada and Public Health Agency of Canada.

T: Take some time to look for organisations practising and advocating public engagement in your area. As well as information and resources, they might also offer networking opportunities that will allow you to meet and talk to people who are already delivering public engagement activities.

T: Lots of these organisations, and others, highlight their public engagement work on social media. By following them you can see what kinds of projects they're working on and how they're delivering public engagement to achieve their goals.

TASK: Find some examples of public engagement by other organisations. Is there anything they have in common? What makes them successful or makes them an example of best practice? Are there any other ideas or pointers that might be useful for your project or area of work? Have you come across any bad 'public engagement' examples? What can you learn from these? For example, are there any pitfalls you might want to look out for in your own work?

5
PLAN AND PREPARE

Public engagement requires a great deal of planning and there are often many strands to keep track of, so it will be essential to get organised.

Tip 35: Use project-planning tools to organise your public engagement activities

T: Over the page, you will find an example worksheet that helps you to develop the plan for your public engagement activities. It sets out the key elements to cover in your initial planning and prompts you to start thinking about the detail.

T: It will also be important, and necessary, to employ other organisational and project planning tools. For example: to map out the details and timings of activities; capture information about, or input from, your target audience, key stakeholders, and other sources; design survey questions or baseline study strategies. You'll also need more detailed plans for each aspect of the activity, for instance, event plans and your detailed evaluation plan. And make sure you keep all these plans and sources of information in one place. The essential thing is to make sure you plan and prepare well.

T: Keeping your information together and connected to the main plan will make it a lot easier to ensure that all your research and upfront thinking genuinely informs what you do. It will also help you to monitor your progress and to carry out a thorough and honest evaluation at the end.

Example planning worksheet:

Project summary
Briefly describe your project or what your area of work is about

How will outside perspectives support your work?

One-off engagement activity or ongoing?

Project aim
State what outcome you want to achieve

Is the goal to consult or collaborate?

Objectives
List specific, measurable steps that will help you achieve your aim

Target audience
Identify the group(s) of people you want to engage with or involve

Where will you find your audience(s)?

What is the role and goal of each group?

How will you work with them?

Stakeholders
Identify and map key stakeholders

How and what you will communicate with each of them?

Activity planning
Note down the approach(es) that might be a good starting point

What further insight or input do you need to refine your plans?

What will you need to deliver the activity? Where and when will it need to take place?

Are there any additional considerations?

Evaluation
Outline how you will monitor and measure the impact of your activity

- Output measures
- Outcome measures

Planning notes
Add further notes to inform your plan

(add links to documents, spreadsheets and charts that provide the detail)

For example:
- Timelines
- Details of participants
- Required resources
- Stakeholder map
- Evaluation plan

FINAL WORD

Now you've come to the end of our tips, you should be well equipped to propel your public engagement activity to the next level. If you follow the five key fundamentals we've covered here, your public engagement will have the best chance of success and impact. It's all about planning, really listening to your target audience, and allowing them to help shape your work every step of the way. It might take more effort, but taking the plunge and doing it right can reap great rewards.

So, take your time, be patient and enjoy the journey. Good luck!

NOTES

NOTES

NOTES

NOTES

NOTES

NOTES

NOTES

CPSIA information can be obtained
at www.ICGtesting.com
Printed in the USA
BVHW040404070321
601818BV00031B/1580

9 781034 006138